EDIE KINSMAN

NLP SECRETS

Unveiling the Powerful Techniques of Neuro-Linguistic Programming for Personal Growth and Success (2024)

Contents

1

INTRODUCTION

Congratulations on your purchase of NLP, and we sincerely thank you for choosing it.

Have you ever longed for a user manual for your mind? Perhaps you've wished for the ability to observe and transform the way you communicate with others. Maybe you're seeking better strategies to address personal challenges, or you've recognized the need for substantial shifts in your worldview but are unsure where to begin.

Fortunately, despite the intricate nature of the human mind, there are methods to tap into its potential. You can acquire the skills to navigate the world more effectively, gain mastery over self-control, and delve into your own mental landscape. You can uncover the innate programming within your mind and leverage it to influence your behavior, effectively programming yourself through techniques like neurolinguistic programming.

This book will guide you in doing just that. You'll learn how to access your unconscious mind, the driving force behind your actions, and use it to enhance self-motivation. By communicating with your mind in a way it understands, you'll regain meaningful control over your life. All you need to do is learn the language of programming your brain demands.

Broadly, NLP has its origins in therapeutic applications, designed to enable practitioners without formal psychology training to assist clients in reprogramming their minds. It involves tapping into the mind, identifying programming issues, and rewriting them to better cope with challenges.

In this book, we'll begin by defining NLP and exploring its numerous advantages for taking charge of your mind. We'll examine its common applications and contexts where it can be employed. Essential principles and foundational knowledge will be discussed before delving into the core workings of NLP. Mind mapping will take center stage as the primary component shaping your perceptions of the world, along with a focus on the unconscious mind's pivotal role in NLP.

Next, we'll get down to business. You'll be guided on how NLP can empower you to improve yourself and extend its use for influencing others in various settings. You'll discover how NLP can unlock the minds of others, provided you establish rapport effectively. Sensory cues employed by people will be explained, and you'll receive instruction on several NLP techniques for both personal and interpersonal use.

Regardless of your background, life journey, or current circumstances, there are pathways to overcome challenges. You can gradually regain control, learn to manage your reactions, and understand how to harness your own mind, as well as influence the minds of others. With the knowledge presented in this book, you'll have the tools to take charge of yourself permanently. All you need to do is read it.

2

NEURO-LINGUISTIC PROGRAMMING

At some juncture in your life, you've likely harbored the desire to transform yourself. Perhaps you grappled with an unpleasant habit you wished to shed. Maybe you yearned for greater self-motivation to stay on course and accomplish your goals. It's possible that you frequently find yourself ensnared in unfavorable situations due to unyielding thought patterns. These habits can embed themselves so deeply that breaking free seems inconceivable. It becomes difficult to envision a life outside the confines of these familiar routines. When habits become second nature, they exert a powerful hold, making it challenging to perceive alternatives or escape their grip.

However, there's encouraging news: just as you can fall into detrimental habits over time, you can also acquire new ones. You can learn to recognize your typical interactions with the world and train yourself to respond differently. This concept is not novel; it has been applied in various contexts. Cognitive behavioral therapy, a widely-praised psychotherapeutic approach known for its quick results with minimal effort, has gained recognition for its capacity for cognitive restructuring, essentially rewiring the mind. Similarly, other therapies incorporate analogous principles.

Neuro-Linguistic Programming (NLP) possesses its own principles, enabling it to achieve a comparable effect. If you harbor fears or persist in negative habits, such as pushing people away or grappling with anxiety, NLP offers a promising avenue for transformation.

Numerous methods are at your disposal to address a range of issues, be it anxiety, depression, anger, or underlying problems. NLP seeks out these issues, identifies them, and offers strategies for resolution. Ultimately, NLP equips you with a toolkit of coping mechanisms to safeguard your mental well-being and promote success in your pursuits.

As your proficiency in NLP grows, you gain insight into how your mind operates and how to program it to your advantage. Rather than constantly attempting to override your natural thought processes, you learn to work in harmony with your brain's innate functions. When executed correctly, this approach often leads to improved mental functioning, problem resolution, and a winning mindset, all stemming from an understanding of the language of your mind.

Introducing Neuro-Linguistic Programming

A fundamental tenet of NLP is acknowledging that you lack control over external factors. You cannot determine whether the car in the adjacent lane will suddenly swerve, whether your home will be vandalized overnight, or if your child will adhere to their bedtime. Accepting this fact is essential; you must be willing to contend with it. Recognizing what falls within your sphere of control versus what doesn't can reshape your thinking, leading to more productive behaviors. By understanding your realm of influence, you can fine-tune your mindset and cultivate the desired behaviors.

In essence, this concept revolves around the interplay of thoughts, emotions, and actions. It's a fundamental principle shared by various behavioral therapies, including NLP. When you apply these methods, you begin to exert control over yourself by comprehending the intricate workings of your mind. Essentially, your thoughts about a particular matter give rise to emotions, which, in turn, influence your behavior. Often, these behaviors reinforce your initial thoughts, creating a cycle that must be addressed to regain control.

NLP heavily relies on this principle. It posits that your thoughts typically stem from past experiences, whether traumatic or enjoyable. Regardless of the source, the outcome remains consistent: a foundational thought underpins your actions in relation to it. This thought shapes your behavior, becoming the core element that permeates everything else.

Let's place this situation in context for a moment. Picture yourself in a severe car accident caused by a drunk driver. Fortunately, both of you survived, but you endured an extended hospital recovery and now have a permanently injured knee. This knee constantly aches, and there's nothing you can do to change that. The aftermath of the accident has left you with a deeply negative association with driving. Your mind links driving to the pain and fear of that accident, along with all the subsequent troubles: the year of physical therapy, attempts at recovery, medical bills, and more. Although you're immensely grateful to be alive, your unconscious mind doesn't see it that way. When you see a car, you don't think about your good fortune; instead, you visualize the accident.

Such trauma often follows accidents or other traumatic events, trapping you in a negative mindset. Negative beliefs continually resurface whenever you confront the situation. For instance, as soon as you get into a car, those same thoughts from your recovery period flood your mind. It's beyond your control; your brain has wired itself this way.

However, there's a way to regain control. Neuro-Linguistic Programming (NLP) acknowledges the immense power of your thoughts. The placebo effect in medical trials demonstrates the influence of thoughts – some individuals who receive a placebo, essentially a sugar pill, report symptom improvement and better thought control. This phenomenon is so common that during labor or cancer treatment, individuals are encouraged to maintain a positive mindset, as it's crucial for recovery. When people genuinely believe they can recover and thrive, they are more capable of coping.

NLP is centered on this principle. It focuses on helping individuals establish positive, empowering beliefs as the foundation for everything they do. When positivity underlies your thoughts, your behavior naturally aligns with it. If you believe you can achieve something, you're more likely to put in the effort because you have faith in your capabilities. Learning to shift your thinking in this way enables you to better cope and take control of your mind.

The Mind, the Body, and You

NLP recognizes the close connection between the mind and the body. Together, they form your identity, like two sides of the same coin, intricately linked yet distinct. You possess both the conscious mind, which you control, and the unconscious mind, which operates beyond your control. These two aspects of the mind are vital, but they often struggle to communicate and align. You may want to drive again after your accident, but your unconscious mind, operating based on its current paradigm, generates fear instead. When you sit behind the wheel, fear overwhelms you, and your unconscious mind doesn't understand that it's not fulfilling your true desires.

The pathway to the unconscious mind often involves the body. By observing body language, including your own, you can gain insight into what the unconscious mind is thinking or doing. Recognizing how your unconscious mind influences your body language and vice versa is a key aspect of NLP. This understanding enables you to bridge the gap between conscious and unconscious thoughts.

In fact, NLP frequently utilizes techniques such as mirroring and pacing, which rely heavily on body language. Building rapport and anchoring, common NLP practices, also involve body language.

Unconscious communication through body language is typically read by the unconscious mind. Understanding this unconscious communication allows you to adjust your actions, interact effectively with others, and establish the right connections.

Neuro-Linguistic Programming Defined

NLP can be dissected into three core processes that define it. Understanding these three components is essential to grasp what NLP is and its potential benefits.

1. Neuro refers to the brain's internal wiring and the nervous system. It encompasses the processing of our five natural senses and how we interpret the world around us. It represents our experiences and how our bodies perceive external interactions, like processing the car accident or recalling

feelings during a difficult conversation.

2. Linguistic pertains to the communication system within your mind. It involves the words, emotions, images, and other senses that your unconscious mind uses to assign value and meaning to experiences. For instance, it may lead you to associate seeing a car with knee pain due to the accident.

3. Programming involves using this information to communicate within yourself. It influences your internal dialogue and behavior. For instance, if your unconscious mind associates cars with fear to keep you safe, you might experience anxiety when considering getting into a car again.

In essence, NLP considers the culmination of your senses, the words you use to describe experiences, and your responses to the world around you. These elements shape your behavior. NLP acknowledges that you have some degree of control, especially over the linguistic aspect. By altering your perspective, you can change your behavior. Taking control of your emotions empowers you to tackle challenges, overcome negativity, and align your programming with your desired outcomes.

3

THE BENEFITS OF NLP

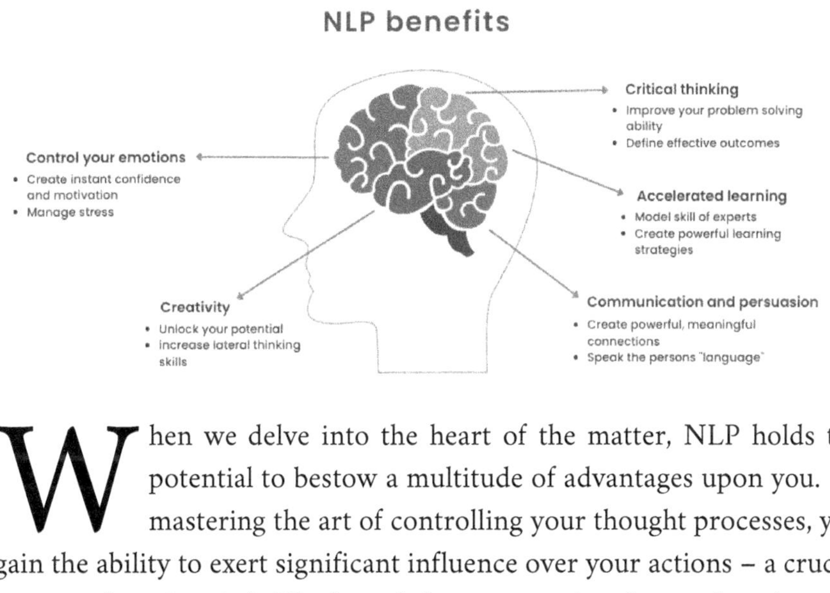

"When we delve into the heart of the matter, NLP holds the potential to bestow a multitude of advantages upon you. By mastering the art of controlling your thought processes, you gain the ability to exert significant influence over your actions – a crucial aspect to bear in mind. The knowledge you acquire about enhancing self-control ensures that, ultimately, you become the person you aspire to be. You can educate yourself to navigate life in accordance with the thought patterns that resonate with your core values. In this way, you fortify yourself to confront any challenges that come your way, yielding profound empowerment. This is a resource you can fully harness to craft the life you

9

desire.

However, in this chapter, we will delve into the finer details. We will explore the myriad ways NLP can be profoundly advantageous to individuals as a whole. Whether you choose to apply NLP techniques to yourself or those around you, remember that these principles remain steadfast. Keep them in your mental toolkit as potential strategies to enhance your own life or to gain insights into how these methods could serve as a wellspring of inspiration.

It Can Sharpen Your Focus

When it boils down to it, NLP has the potential to sharpen your focus – not your physical eyesight, but your ability to hone in on your true desires. It clears the fog from your aspirational vision, allowing you to gain crystal clarity about what you genuinely want in life. You can pinpoint the goals you aspire to achieve and integrate them into your daily existence. Moreover, you can decipher those subconscious behavioral patterns that underlie your actions, and once understood, you can leverage them to your advantage.

In particular, as you become proficient in NLP, you can concentrate on goals that align with a precise purpose. Employing these methods usually ensures their realization. You can typically guarantee that, ultimately, you exercise better self-control. You learn to comprehend how you interact with both yourself and those in your sphere. You learn to navigate toward your goals, and because you have articulated them, you are more likely to achieve them.

It Can Liberate You from Limiting Beliefs

To some extent, we all harbor limiting beliefs – those negative convictions that hold us back. Perhaps you believe you're worthless or incapable of achieving your dreams. It could be another belief entirely, but it shackles your potential.

Let's revisit the example of a hypothetical car accident. In the aftermath, the limiting belief might revolve around the accident itself, instilling an irrational fear of getting back behind the wheel. This belief lurks in the background, hindering self-control and exacerbating problems.

No matter the nature of your limiting belief, NLP equips you with the tools to overcome it. NLP focuses on reframing your existing beliefs, often by altering the meaning you ascribe to events. It involves a linguistic component, but through this linguistic transformation, you can dismantle the negativity that impedes your progress. NLP guides you in tweaking your mindset just enough to ensure that, ultimately, you gain better control. It ensures that, in the end, you possess the capability to reshape your perception of the world, facilitating the necessary changes in your life.

It Can Foster Self-Confidence

Engaging with NLP can effectively address issues of self-confidence. Many individuals, especially those grappling with overwhelmingly negative mindsets, struggle with low self-esteem. Yet, as you take command of your mental processes, you can move forward with newfound confidence. You realize that you have the power to change your thoughts and, consequently, your actions. You grasp that you wield the ability to maintain control over yourself, becoming the sole arbiter of your beliefs. You take the reins, ensuring that your mindset serves your best interests.

In the end, you learn to trust yourself to make sound decisions. You trust that, ultimately, you are capable of making the right choices with ease. This confidence can also be anchored, a technique that enables you to trigger specific emotional states at will. Essentially, you seize control of your interactions, decisively dictating your behavior in alignment with your goals. This self-guidance proves immensely empowering."

It Can Aid You in Handling Challenging Individuals

An essential point to keep in mind is that employing NLP helps you gain a deeper understanding of yourself. It teaches you to recognize that often, how we engage with others holds significance, and you have the option not to react to people with the same intense anger you might have felt before. We all encounter individuals we don't particularly like, whether they're colleagues we interact with regularly or occasional acquaintances. Regardless of the situation, it's vital to comprehend how to manage yourself effectively. When you grasp the art of handling your emotions and coping with yourself, you can fundamentally change your perspective on the people in your life, even those who used to irritate you. You can learn to tolerate them, and in the process, gain a deeper respect for them.

Furthermore, NLP revolves around fostering rapport—an invaluable skill that you'll need to ensure you can control your behavior. By delving into NLP, you can acquire the tools to connect with difficult individuals and apply those techniques to establish rapport with someone who may not initially like you. This can be immensely helpful in cultivating positive relationships with others.

It Can Enhance Your Leadership Abilities

NLP is particularly beneficial for anyone in a leadership role. If you're responsible for leading or guiding others in any capacity, mastering NLP can equip you with the essential skills needed to earn respect. You develop the capabilities required to ensure that people view you as worthy of admiration by establishing your own rapport with them. Additionally, you acquire the ability to discern others' perspectives, which enables you to better handle your interactions with people. These competencies are highly advantageous in leadership positions, and by mastering them, you position yourself for effective leadership.

It Can Foster Problem Solving

NLP is all about fostering creative thinking. It involves taking a problematic thought and finding alternative ways to perceive it. It's akin to looking at a dog and deciding to view it as a four-legged domestic mammal, commonly known as "man's best friend," instead of just a dog. When you alter your definition of something, you can change your reaction to it, which is precisely what NLP aims to achieve.

These problem-solving skills extend beyond NLP and can be applied to various situations. You can employ these methods to develop fresh strategies and novel approaches to different challenges due to the resilience you cultivate through these processes.

It Can Empower You to Control Your Mindset

Similarly, utilizing NLP enables you to take control of your own mind. You gain the ability to command aspects of your life that once seemed beyond your grasp, such as your thoughts and emotions. Many people perceive feelings as automatic and instinctive, seemingly beyond their control. However, it's crucial to remember that your emotions are ultimately products of your thought processes at any given moment. By recognizing this, you can regulate your mindset and emotions. You have the capacity to generate the emotions and motivation necessary to achieve your desired outcomes. When you can change the development of your thoughts and self-improve, you'll discover significant personal growth.

It Can Assist in Breaking Negative Habits

We all grapple with bad habits at some point in our lives, whether it's nail-biting, turning to alcohol on rough workdays, or mindlessly snacking throughout the day. Regardless of the specific habit, it's essential to acknowledge that you possess a degree of control over it. You can learn how to overcome these negative behavioral patterns and eliminate your bad habits. When you achieve this, you ensure that you're not squandering your time, effort, money, or any other resources. Instead, you ensure that you're living the life you desire.

In essence, your bad habits are manifestations of unconscious thoughts being acted out. By identifying these thoughts, reframing them, and taking control of the issue at hand, you can employ various techniques to permanently break these habits.

It Can Improve Your Relationships

Because you invest time in understanding your own nature through NLP, you can foster healthy habits that promote positive relationships. This understanding empowers you to be in complete control of your actions, enabling you to develop constructive habits that enhance both your physical and mental well-being. By doing so, you can ensure that your relationships grow stronger, guided by your improved habits.

It Can Enhance Your Communication Skills

Furthermore, the focus on internal communication in NLP prepares you to better comprehend external communication with others. Consequently, you gain a deeper understanding of how you interact with people. You recognize that your communication doesn't solely affect you; it also influences the way you interact with others, directly impacting them.

This awareness enables you to effectively convey your thoughts and engage with others in a manner that aligns with your objectives. It ensures that your communication is efficient, a skill crucial in all aspects of your social life, which you can develop with NLP as your guide.

It Can Enable You to Assist Others

NLP equips you to help others as well. You can learn how to motivate those around you effectively by identifying their strengths and weaknesses, which enables you to offer valuable support. This involves honing coaching skills that significantly influence others, keeping them motivated. You also acquire the ability to reshape the thoughts of others, a valuable skill. Recognizing how your words can impact others' thoughts and motivations empowers you to guide them effectively.

With this ability, you become capable of assisting people in various contexts, helping them uncover solutions to their most significant challenges. You also gain insight into how they navigate their interactions with others, allowing you to encourage positive changes in their thinking.

It Can Help You Understand Others

You will also develop the capacity to understand and model other people's behaviors. This process, known as modeling, enables you to observe individuals who excel in areas you aspire to, personally or professionally, and emulate their success. By comprehending the factors contributing to their achievements, you can enhance your own capabilities and achieve greater success.

It Can Facilitate Adaptation to Change

NLP equips you to adapt to changes effectively. You become more adaptable and flexible due to your ability to modify your thinking. Instead of solely focusing on the negatives in challenging situations, you learn to identify the positives and adjust how you interact with those around you. You are prepared to cope with any situation that arises, thanks to the NLP techniques you've mastered.

It Can Enhance Workplace Performance

In a professional context, NLP can be a powerful asset. It proves invaluable in managing and motivating teams, ensuring that those you work with maintain a positive attitude, which, in turn, enhances their productivity. It enables you to optimize team performance, run a more efficient operation, and ensure that everyone on your team is contributing effectively.

It Can Simplify Sales and Negotiations

Lastly, NLP offers distinct advantages, especially in sales and negotiation roles. When you're prepared to negotiate, you possess a deep understanding of the dynamics at play. You can negotiate more effectively by employing the skills you've acquired through NLP. You can also better comprehend people by working with the unconscious mind, making interactions with them more manageable. You become more persuasive by framing your communication effectively. Importantly, your intention is not to manipulate but to find common ground and ensure fair agreements. You gain insight into what others want, allowing you to meet their needs and facilitate successful negotiations.

In conclusion, by mastering NLP, you empower yourself to excel in various facets of life, fostering personal growth, enhancing relationships, and achieving professional success.

4

USING NLP

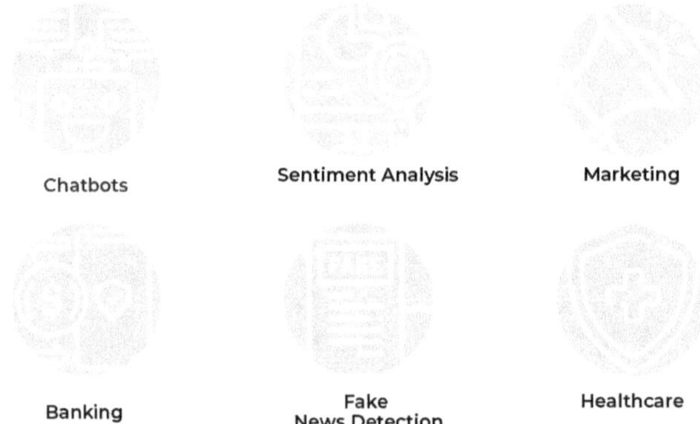

B y the close of the day, Natural Language Processing (NLP) finds utility in a wide array of situations. It is extensively employed in various contexts, each yielding diverse outcomes. Nonetheless, if you aspire to harness the potential of NLP, it is entirely within your control. When you embrace NLP, you can enhance your understanding of your own thoughts and those of others, offering profound insights into the human psyche.

Consequently, NLP can be applied effectively in virtually any social scenario, spanning from parenting and relationships to negotiations. Nevertheless, for the purposes of this chapter, we will narrow our focus. Initially, we will explore the fundamental workings of NLP before delving into its most common applications, such as its role in medicine, self-improvement, interpersonal dynamics, negotiations, workplace dynamics, relationships, and a brief mention of its potential misuse. It's important to note that while NLP can be a powerful tool for positive change, its misuse as a manipulative device is discouraged and should be avoided, as it tarnishes the potential benefits and leads to resistance from some individuals who seek control over their surroundings.

How NLP Functions

In essence, NLP operates according to a straightforward equation:
Input + Internal processes = Output

Your output, encompassing behaviors and emotions, essentially results from the combination of input and internal processes. This simplification aids beginners in grasping the concept. It all begins with the input, which represents the external world. Input encompasses sensory data received by your body, including kinesthetic (related to movement and touch), visual (pertaining to sight), auditory (related to hearing), olfactory (concerning smell), and gustatory (relating to taste) stimuli. These sensory experiences shape your interactions with the world and are processed primarily through your senses.

These senses are subsequently influenced by internal processes, which consist of unconscious filters and internal representations of processed data. These unconscious processes significantly influence your behavior and responses.

The filters act as a metaphorical sieve through which your sensory data is sifted. They draw upon your past experiences to better comprehend your current circumstances. Your unconscious mind forms hypotheses based on background data, and without this information, you cannot make informed judgments. Consequently, you tend to perceive the world based on past experiences. For example, if you've been in a car accident, you might avoid driving on holidays with a high incidence of drunk driving, like the 4th of July, New Year's, Christmas, and Thanksgiving. This avoidance stems from the generalization that holidays are associated with drunk driving incidents—a result of your filters at work.

Filters typically manifest as generalizations, attitudes, memories, thought processes, values, beliefs, strategies, and the language you employ to describe your experiences. After passing through these filters, your sensory inputs are processed by your internal representations.

Ultimately, your output, whether it manifests as emotions or behaviors, is shaped by your experiences and thought processes, creating a chain of cause and effect.

In essence, NLP seeks to modify these filters or influence your internal representations, thereby altering your behavior. By adapting your internal processes to align with your objectives, your output changes accordingly, enabling you to effectively utilize NLP.

NLP in Medicine

NLP is occasionally promoted as a remedy for various illnesses, including cancer and HIV, which require medical treatment. While NLP is not a panacea, it can assist in mitigating the psychological effects of enduring chronic or terminal diseases. When employed during critical illness, NLP aids individuals in accepting their conditions, processing information more effectively, and adopting a mindset conducive to coping with their challenges.

It is crucial to emphasize that NLP does not cure diseases like cancer, HIV, or AIDS. It is not a form of medicine in itself. Instead, it serves as a potent tool, akin to meditation, mindfulness, and various therapies employed by individuals facing illness. NLP can be a valuable adjunct during illness but should not replace conventional medical treatment.

Neuro-Linguistic Programming (NLP) finds extensive application in psychotherapy, originally conceived as a streamlined approach to therapy requiring less training. It effectively addresses common mental health concerns such as negative emotions, anxiety, depression, and other psychological issues by focusing on altering thought patterns. NLP follows a systemic, solution-focused approach, enabling individuals to reframe unhelpful thoughts.

In essence, NLP aligns with the objectives of various solution-focused brief therapies, pinpointing issues for resolution. This process empowers individuals to resolve problems, subsequently witnessing the desired behavioral changes. The strength of NLP lies in its ability to restore personal agency, allowing clients to treat themselves by gaining a profound understanding of their inner workings. Armed with this knowledge, individuals are better equipped to navigate life's challenges.

NLP for Self-Improvement

A recurring theme in NLP applications centers on self-improvement. When individuals concentrate on self-development, they can reshape their mindsets. NLP serves as a potent tool for self-improvement, gradually eliminating negative issues and fostering a life of personal value. By harnessing NLP, people can gain mastery over their thought processes, discard detrimental habits, and eradicate self-sabotaging thoughts, ultimately evolving into their fullest potential.

NLP in Leadership and Management

NLP is also frequently employed in managerial roles, enabling individuals to influence and motivate others effectively. Whether in leadership positions or team dynamics, NLP techniques assist in optimizing interactions and ensuring efficient teamwork. Employing NLP as a leadership tool empowers individuals to guide others towards desired outcomes, enhancing overall efficiency.

NLP in Negotiation and Persuasion

In the realm of negotiation, NLP proves highly effective, especially when negotiations begin on a challenging note. Skillful use of NLP techniques can encourage openness and willingness to negotiate, even in initially resistant parties. By skillfully framing questions and understanding the perspectives of others, NLP can be a powerful asset in achieving desired outcomes during negotiations.

NLP in Relationships

In relationships, NLP offers a valuable toolkit for fostering connections. It helps individuals approach situations in ways that naturally facilitate relationship growth. Utilizing NLP in relationships enhances communication and provides insights into the dynamics of interpersonal interactions. This fosters rapport, trust, and deeper connections with others.

NLP and Manipulation

Regrettably, NLP can also be misused for manipulation, a darker context compared to its other applications. In such cases, individuals exploit NLP's persuasive power for their personal gain, disregarding the principles of growth and help it was intended for. It is crucial to remember that NLP itself is morally neutral; its ethical implications depend on how individuals employ it. The responsibility lies with the user, not the technique itself.

5

THE PRINCIPLES OF NLP AND OTHER ESSENTIAL INFORMATION

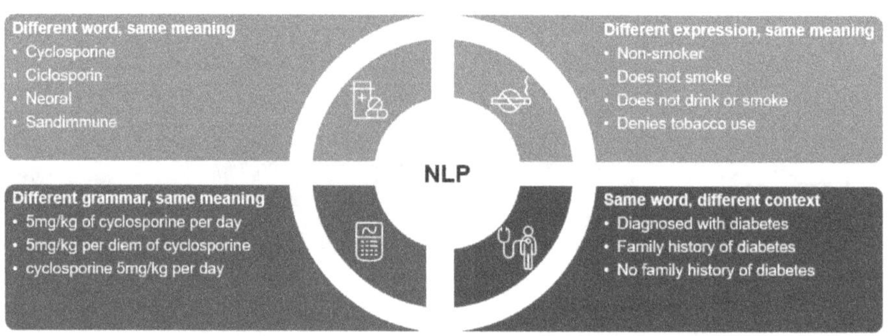

Before delving into the more critical information that will equip you to utilize the techniques within this book, it is essential to grasp the guiding principles of NLP. These principles constitute a blend of core concepts recurring throughout the book and the four fundamental pillars that shape your engagement with NLP. These pillars wield substantial influence and offer insight into the objectives underlying your use of NLP. Additionally, the introduced concepts will clarify the specific targets you'll address to effectively tackle the challenges at hand.

This chapter places a strong emphasis on furnishing the foundational knowledge necessary for your journey. It's imperative to acknowledge the significance of this chapter, as it lays the groundwork for comprehending the forthcoming content. In essence, your comprehension of these principles is pivotal; failure to grasp and retain them will likely hinder your progress in subsequent sections of this book, posing a substantial obstacle for most individuals. Therefore, investing the time to thoroughly grasp the content and recognize its purpose is crucial to your ultimate success.

The Pillars of NLP

Before we embark on this journey, it's crucial to recognize that, like any other concept or therapy, NLP is built upon a bedrock of background information. These concepts provide the necessary support, giving NLP its focus and delineating its objectives. NLP mirrors other fields of thought and therapeutic methods in its reliance on key concepts that profoundly shape one's worldview. These concepts dictate how you perceive and act upon the world, elucidating NLP's underlying motivations.

For practitioners of NLP, four key points demand your constant attention. By keeping these four factors in mind, you can ensure your success and effectively harness NLP's power. These four defining factors serve as your guideposts, enabling you to influence others according to your intentions: Rapport, sensory awareness, outcome thinking, and behavioral flexibility.

Rapport

The foremost pillar of NLP is rapport. It serves as the cornerstone upon which everything else is built. Without establishing rapport with someone, the application of NLP techniques becomes a daunting endeavor. Rapport functions as the magical ingredient that makes NLP work; it's the force that allows you to shape others' thoughts and behaviors. Essentially, it measures the level of trust between you and another individual.

Rapport typically develops organically over time. Observe two close friends, and you'll notice the synergy in their body language. They are attuned to each other, engaging in mirroring—unconsciously aligning their body language to better understand one another. This phenomenon stems from the activation of mirror neurons in the brain, which fire when we observe someone else's actions. It's how we empathize with others and discern their emotional states.

Generally, the stronger the rapport between individuals, the more profound their mutual empathy, leading to increased activation of mirror neurons and a greater tendency for the brain to mimic each other's behaviors.

Next time you're at a restaurant, observe couples who are clearly in long-term relationships. Notice how their movements seem synchronized, with one often following the lead of the other, even in simple actions like taking a drink. This natural harmony is a testament to the trust they share.

Contrast this with a couple on an awkward first date, uncertain of their compatibility. Their behaviors appear disjointed as if they inhabit different worlds.

Rapport acts as a tangible indicator of trustworthiness. Once you recognize its presence, you can easily identify it and pinpoint areas where you can enhance your interactions. This heightened awareness helps you navigate situations more effectively and gauge whether someone is receptive enough for you to employ NLP techniques.

We will delve deeper into rapport in Chapter 9: Rapport. For now, understand that it constitutes a vital component of NLP, especially if you intend to apply NLP techniques on others. In such cases, you will need to adhere to specific protocols outlined later in the book.

Sensory Awareness

The second foundational pillar of NLP is sensory awareness. This principle underscores the notion that every interaction and communication with others hinges on our senses. You must keenly observe how those around you engage their senses, discerning which senses they favor and which they pay less attention to. Being attuned to your surroundings is paramount.

If you intend to employ NLP techniques on others, there are myriad factors to consider. Contemplate the environment in which you wish to apply these techniques. Reflect on your interactions with others and adapt your presentation to align with their sensory preferences. If you are employing NLP for personal growth, you must also recognize your own sensory inclinations. Understanding how you engage with your senses and interact with the world around you is essential for effectively addressing any challenges that may arise during your journey.

To effectively utilize NLP for yourself or others, it's essential to recognize nonverbal cues, whether they are your own or someone else's. This awareness plays a crucial role in ensuring that body language aligns with your communication goals. You can harness this sensory awareness to identify your own emotions, such as anger or anxiety, and leverage that understanding to your advantage. Similarly, you can use it to gauge the emotions of others and explore how the environment contributes to these feelings. This ability not only grants you better control over situations but also provides valuable insights for future use.

Outcome thinking, the third pillar of NLP, revolves around setting and achieving goals. Every interaction becomes an opportunity to work toward a specific objective. It involves pinpointing goals that motivate and guide your actions, ensuring that any influence you exert on someone's mindset, whether yours or another's, remains intentional and purpose-driven. Many people falter when they lack clear goals to propel them forward. Well-defined goals enable you to identify precisely what needs to change in someone else's thinking or your own, directing your reframing efforts toward successful outcomes.

Ultimately, your goal can vary widely, but you must prioritize it and allow it to be the driving force behind your actions. Flexibility in behavior, the fourth pillar, entails having multiple strategies at your disposal and adapting your interactions to suit different situations and individuals. It means being willing to abandon ineffective approaches and pivot when necessary, ensuring that you always find a solution, even if it's not your initial choice.

Additionally, flexibility fosters resilience, preventing you from succumbing to the temptation to give up or accept defeat. When dealing with the human mind, rigid thinking won't suffice. You must embrace significant changes and persevere through obstacles. Only then can these principles truly work for you.

In addition to the fundamental pillars of NLP, three core concepts—subjectivity, consciousness, and learning—are crucial for understanding how to influence others' minds effectively. Subjectivity acknowledges that everyone perceives the world uniquely, influenced by their experiences and perspectives. This individuality shapes how people interpret and react to situations, and it's essential to respect and work with these varying viewpoints.

Consciousness, the second concept, distinguishes between the conscious and unconscious mind. The conscious mind is what you're aware of—your active thoughts and feelings—while the unconscious operates beyond your immediate awareness, governing automatic patterns. NLP can help rewrite the unconscious mind, a topic explored in later chapters.

Learning, the final concept, is the driving force behind NLP. It centers on acquiring new behaviors and thought patterns, whether for yourself or others. Recognizing that behaviors and thoughts are learned allows for their rewriting and improvement. NLP leverages the learning process, often through modeling the behaviors and thought patterns of others.

In summary, these principles and concepts are fundamental to mastering NLP and effectively influencing the minds of individuals. Understanding subjectivity, consciousness, and learning, along with the four pillars of NLP, empowers you to navigate the intricacies of human interaction and communication successfully.

6

MAPS, THE MIND, AND NLP

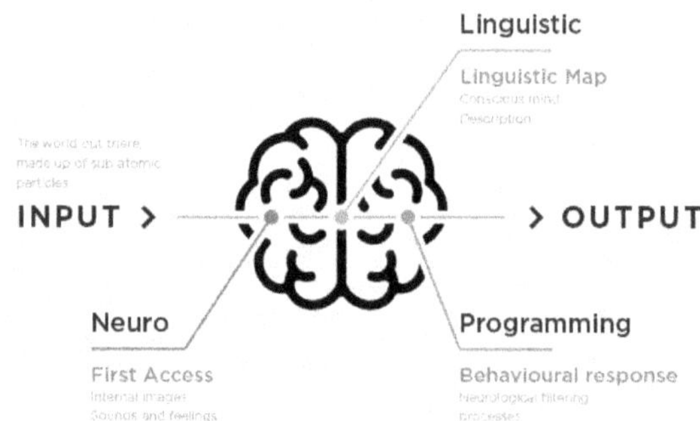

s we've previously established, our understanding of the world plays a pivotal role in shaping our lives. It influences our interactions with the environment, our emotional responses, behaviors, and inclinations. Essentially, it governs our identity and actions, thanks to the mental maps that act as our guiding compass. These mental maps wield immense power, and mastering them is tantamount to gaining control over our minds.

In this chapter, we will delve deep into this concept. We will explore how one can influence the minds of others, as well as their own. It's crucial to recognize that, ultimately, we are controlled by the mental maps we live by. These maps dictate how we perceive our actions and how we fit into the fabric of reality. They serve as our navigational tools, guiding us seamlessly through life's myriad situations. They define our world, facilitating our comprehension of everything around us, all without the need for conscious deliberation. After all, why pause to assess the potential danger of a snake when you could already be bitten? Sometimes, swift action trumps contemplation in matters of survival.

This discussion relies heavily on generalizations, a theme we will thoroughly explore in this chapter. We will examine how these generalizations and perceptions form the maps that enable us to navigate the world. Furthermore, we will investigate the relationship between these mental maps and the application of Neuro-Linguistic Programming (NLP), whether on ourselves or on others. As you progress through this chapter, you will gain insights into how people perceive the world, fostering a better understanding of how others interact with their surroundings and how you relate to both yourself and the world at large.

Our Perceptions of Reality

In our lives, we are continually inundated with sensory experiences. Your reality, from your unique vantage point, differs significantly from that of someone standing beside you. Irrespective of your location, circumstances, or identity, your perspective undergoes constant transformation, molded by the world's stimuli and your explorations within it. Understanding why you perceive the world the way you do hinges on learning how to decipher these mental maps.

Your senses continuously gather data, even if you're not consciously aware of it. The unconscious mind, a topic we'll explore in the next chapter, remains highly perceptive, registering everything within your sensory realm. Even when you're not actively focusing on it, your unconscious mind acknowledges its presence. Consider this: Have you ever conversed with someone in a park and instinctively ducked when a ball hurtled towards you? Although you may not have consciously noticed the ball, your unconscious mind was vigilant about your surroundings, prompting your reflexive reaction. This automatic response extends to other potential threats, such as spiders, snakes, or any dangers in your environment.

These perceptions can swiftly transcend mere sensory input to become patterns of recognition. Imagine you're in a relationship where your interactions adapt to the dynamic. Perhaps your partner consistently displays signs of disappointment—audible sighs, slumped shoulders, and a look of annoyance—whenever you make a mistake or express differing opinions. While you might not consciously recognize this pattern, your unconscious mind is paying attention. It recognizes this recurring behavior and associates your errors or misunderstandings with disappointing others. This may not surface in your conscious thoughts, yet every mistake reinforces the notion that you've let down those around you. You internalize the need to alter your interactions, all unbeknownst to your conscious mind.

Your perception of reality is constructed upon a foundation of automatic thoughts like these. It's shaped by observing how others react to your actions and adapting to various situations. Every experience contributes to your evolving understanding of how to navigate the world. From your upbringing to the challenges you've faced, these experiences mold your perception and influence your interactions with the world. If you've had experiences that instill a fear of spiders, every encounter with one will trigger a response as if it were a terrifying threat. It could be a past spider bite, witnessing someone else's panic, or simply learning that spiders are dangerous that initially formed this perception of reality and fear.

In fact, you form perceptions about nearly everything you encounter. People tend to form judgments about the world they experience, even if they don't readily admit it. Constant evaluations are made and applied, quickly giving rise to mental images of the world and how it functions. This is a crucial point to acknowledge. When you recognize these processes at work, you gain insight into how you engage with the world and how your navigational tools, composed of judgments and perceptions, come together to create your mental maps.

The Concept of Mental Mapping

When you compile all your perceptions of reality, you create what is referred to as mental maps. Continuously, you engage in mental mapping, which involves constructing a framework for navigating the world around you. These maps serve as guides to help you better comprehend the world and how you navigate your experiences within it.

In essence, you shape your interactions with the world based on these mental maps. They provide insights into how you should adapt to the world around you. When you navigate the world based on the mental maps you create, you are essentially following a predetermined path.

Remember that these mental maps are the internal processes that influence your behavior. They determine the way you interact with the world, and your instinctive reactions are influenced by the perceptions you accumulate over time. Ultimately, these mental maps define who you are and your tendencies as you navigate the world.

To ensure healthy behaviors, it's crucial to ensure that your mental maps are sound.

Furthermore, these mental maps reside within your unconscious mind. They exist just beneath the surface of your conscious awareness, allowing you to tap into them. To gain a deeper understanding of yourself and modify your thought patterns, you must pause and reflect on the world around you.

NLP and the Use of Mental Maps

Fortunately, it is relatively simple to influence the development of mental maps. Whether you aim to influence your own mental maps or those of others, the fundamental concept remains the same: you constantly reside within your own mental map. Your perceptions of reality continuously shape the world you inhabit, and expecting otherwise would be unrealistic. It's essential to acknowledge that your perception of the world differs inherently from that of your neighbor due to your unique life experiences and upbringing. This divergence can complicate your understanding of others, as no two people will share the exact same mindset, making true agreement challenging.

This divergence can also lead to other problems. When someone's mental map is heavily skewed by past traumas or issues, how can it be rectified? How can you begin to mend these distorted beliefs or images to prevent negative influences? How can you help yourself or others establish a healthy mental map?

Ultimately, you can learn how to influence these mental maps. You can learn to change the way you interact with the world and modify these mental maps, whether through coaching or other methods. This allows you to regulate your interactions more effectively. There are several key approaches to influencing your own or others' mental maps.

Firstly, you can focus on expanding these mental maps. If they have developed within a narrow context, you can work to broaden them, enabling more effective learning. By closely examining how you perceive the world and your interactions within it, you can identify and rectify issues. Expanding your mental maps beyond their narrow confines can dilute negative or problematic perceptions.

Secondly, you can work within your existing mental map. Instead of trying to expand it, you can address the situation from within, determining how to effect change. Gaining control of your surroundings allows you to influence the mental map effectively. As you gain this influence, you develop the necessary understanding for a successful mindset.

Finally, you can also employ other NLP techniques, which may not be designed explicitly to influence mental maps but can certainly do so. By using NLP for personal development, you can enhance your mindset's flexibility and control your thought processes, adapting to more beneficial mental maps.

In conclusion, you can evaluate the constructiveness of your mental map through self-reflection or by observing others and their mental maps. The simplest reflection involves assessing whether your worldview brings joy and fulfillment to your life. Does it foster happiness and satisfaction, or does it make you feel trapped and in conflict?

With an inefficient mental map, you or others will struggle to lead a happy and healthy life. It's not a reflection of personal shortcomings but rather a consequence of having a skewed worldview. To truly find comfort in your own skin and the world around you, you must learn to realign your worldview.

7

THE UNCONSCIOUS MIND

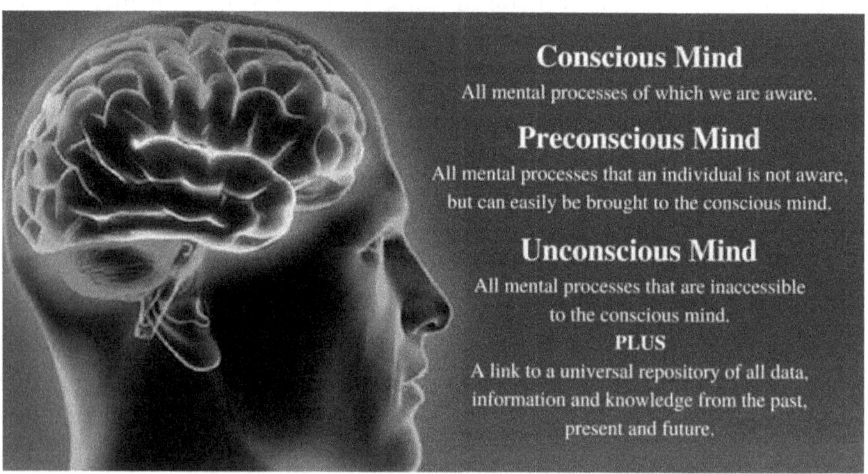

Beneath the surface of your identity lies the subconscious mind, a silent orchestrator that plays a pivotal role in your daily interactions with the world. It serves as the mechanism through which you exercise control over your behavior. In essence, it is the processing hub for all that transpires within your psyche.

The subconscious mind operates seamlessly, ensuring your continued breathing during sleep and your responsiveness to the external environment. It acts as a guardian, preventing detrimental actions and crafting emotions to convey ideas to your conscious mind. This covert conductor controls your impulses and innate desires, compelling you to engage more effectively with those around you. It wields dominion over virtually all your actions, making it the linchpin in determining your behaviors and life choices.

In navigating life's journey, your subconscious mind assumes the role of your guide, safeguarding you from peril and identifying potential issues to influence your behavior for your protection. It helps you avoid remorse for your actions. While you may not consciously perceive its presence, it wields greater influence than other facets of your mind. Despite your familiarity with conscious learning, your awareness is limited to only a portion of your mental realm, concealing a vast, uncharted territory beneath the surface.

Much like an iceberg, the conscious mind represents only a fraction of what defines you, with the bulk of your essence residing in the realm of unconscious thoughts. Acknowledging this reality prompts mindfulness toward your subconscious musings, revealing the substantial reservoir of untapped mental potential beneath the conscious mind's veneer. In fact, more than 90% of your mental faculties remain dormant, lurking beneath the surface.

Distinguishing the Conscious from the Unconscious Mind

The conscious mind operates within the realm of awareness. It comes into play when you deliberate on complex behaviors and cognitive processes, constituting the portion of your mental faculties you consciously engage. While it garners your immediate attention, it does not constitute the majority of your mental processing. The conscious mind governs conscious thought, logical and critical thinking, long-term memory, and the willpower needed to resist undesirable impulses.

It is crucial to recognize that you do maintain awareness of your conscious actions. However, beneath this conscious layer, a complex web of automatic thoughts, habits, emotions, and more continually unfolds. These automatic processes require less cognitive capacity, as conscious thinking demands heightened attention and awareness.

Imagine having to consciously deliberate every single action throughout your day—it would be remarkably inefficient. Consider the simplicity of brushing your teeth, for instance. The process involves applying toothpaste to a toothbrush and brushing, a routine so ingrained that it occurs automatically without conscious effort.

Numerous intricate processes are involved in this, all requiring your attention. It's essential to acknowledge that you exert effort to complete these tasks diligently. Remember the precise movements of your hand, both forward and backward, and be mindful of consciously grasping whatever you hold. Additionally, you need to adapt your arm's motion by engaging different muscles. It would be highly inefficient to consciously activate each muscle group individually, which is why your subconscious mind simplifies this by managing these habits to ensure your well-being.

Similar processes apply to other aspects of your life. Your values, for instance, stem from deeply rooted beliefs that develop over time. These beliefs help you better comprehend your priorities and enable you to make quick judgments about your surroundings. Without these automatic thoughts regarding your beliefs, you may encounter difficulties in understanding situations. For instance, if you believe that all friendly dogs you encounter on the street deserve a pat on the head and a treat, you'll instinctively follow through when you see one. Likewise, if you firmly believe in treating people with respect, you'll naturally do so without conscious thought.

This is the remarkable power of the unconscious mind. It transforms important beliefs into habits, ensuring your satisfaction and reducing the need for conscious deliberation. Acknowledging the significance of your unconscious thoughts is crucial; failing to do so can lead to various problems. Your unconscious thoughts form the foundation of your mental framework, and recognizing this is essential.

The unconscious mind encompasses beliefs, emotions, habitual behaviors, the values you uphold, and intuition. Moreover, it plays a critical role in safeguarding your survival. Consider your visceral responses when feeling threatened or receiving news of failure or betrayal. These gut reactions are also the handiwork of your unconscious mind, designed to protect you.

8

PROGRAMMING YOURSELF

"Programming yourself doesn't have to be a daunting task. It need not be a source of anxiety. With a few simple considerations, you can take full control of your life and shape it according to your desires. In this chapter, we will explore how you can harness this power for yourself, delving into the methods to obtain the power you seek. All you need to do is ensure that you are better equipped to recognize the patterns you need to follow.

Within this chapter, we will address ways to self-program. Often, NLP is acquired and honed with the primary goal of achieving control. It's designed to foster the beliefs and habits necessary for self-mastery. You are the master of your own destiny. You can learn to govern your mind, both the conscious and the unconscious aspects. You can master the patterns that govern your life, rewriting the map once and for all, ensuring that you gain the understanding needed to change yourself, your behaviors, and more. Learning it is straightforward, and as long as you are willing to commit the effort, NLP can become an incredibly valuable tool for your personal development.

NLP Targets:

When it comes to self-programming, there are three ways to significantly aid yourself in becoming the best version of yourself possible. You can cultivate the state you wish to master, work on your personal narrative, and change the strategies by which you navigate life. By focusing on these aspects, you can make the desired changes in your life.

Changing Your State:

NLP primarily focuses on altering your emotional state or mood at any given moment. It's crucial to realize that the way you interact with the world is heavily influenced by your emotional state. Understanding this connection empowers you to figure out how best to change your state. Your emotional state can impact your behaviors, sometimes in problematic ways, which is why it's essential to take control of your mindset. Learning NLP grants you this power.

Changing Your Story:

NLP also helps you transform your life narrative. Often, this narrative can be distorted or negative, affecting your behavior and self-perception. By reframing your story and adjusting the way you talk to yourself, you can work more effectively with others and gain better self-control. Reframing your narrative allows you to align your future behaviors with your desired life goals.

Changing Your Strategy:

Lastly, NLP can assist you in changing your mental strategy or thought process. Your strategy is the mental map you follow, governing your actions and decisions. Regardless of your life goals, changing this strategy can be challenging, but it's entirely achievable. By overcoming ingrained habits, you can begin to alter your behaviors.

The Keys to Self-Development:

To develop yourself, you must implement NLP principles diligently. Your approach to the world around you should align with your goals. Self-development depends on implementing specific patterns and steps to change your thinking and become more positive and effective in life. To achieve this, you must adopt certain keys and make them integral to your life.

Understanding Your Patterns:

Recognizing your current behaviors is crucial. Self-development requires understanding how you behave and identifying problematic habits. Realize that your thoughts lead to feelings, which, in turn, lead to behaviors. By acknowledging this chain, you can identify troublesome habits and pave the way for personal growth.

Changing Your Patterns:

After identifying your patterns, you must learn to modify them. You can either enhance beneficial patterns or work on changing those that hinder your progress. Whether you continue to follow existing behaviors or adapt them to align with your goals, changing patterns is the catalyst for achieving the lifestyle you desire."

Enhance Your Communication Skills

In the process of transforming yourself and altering your habitual behaviors, you'll naturally find that your communication skills improve. The art of effective communication becomes more accessible than ever before, and as you cultivate these improved behaviors, you'll realize that you are better prepared than you initially believed to embrace positive behaviors. Ultimately, successful personal growth hinges on your ability to communicate effectively, both with yourself and with others.

Strive to Accomplish Your Objectives

Another crucial aspect to focus on is the achievement of your goals, which holds significant importance in Neuro-Linguistic Programming (NLP). It's essential to set clear goals and commit to pursuing them diligently. Without this commitment, you may struggle to attain your objectives. However, remember that you can develop the capability to achieve your goals through deliberate effort. By altering your behaviors and nurturing self-motivation, you can become the person you aspire to be. The process of striving to achieve your goals and maintaining a persistent focus on your accomplishments empowers you to thrive, regardless of the life circumstances you encounter.

Understand the Language of Your Mind

You must also pause and familiarize yourself with the language of your mind. Language plays a pivotal role in this journey, and neglecting its significance can hinder your progress. Your success is closely tied to your ability to monitor and comprehend the way your mind communicates with you. To ensure your success, invest the necessary time to comprehend your mind's operations and anticipate your thought patterns. It is crucial to be attuned to the way you talk to yourself if you want to achieve your goals. This entails mastering the use of language and transforming it into a more constructive and empowering internal dialogue.

Strive for Continuous Self-Improvement

Lastly, remember that continuous self-improvement should be your ultimate endeavor. Approach every aspect of your life with the mindset of perpetual enhancement. Maintain the belief that you can always improve, and that you will indeed improve. Fostering this mindset is imperative, as failing to do so can impede your progress. Recognize that the way you manage yourself and your self-perception significantly influences your overall success.

9

PROGRAMMING OTHERS

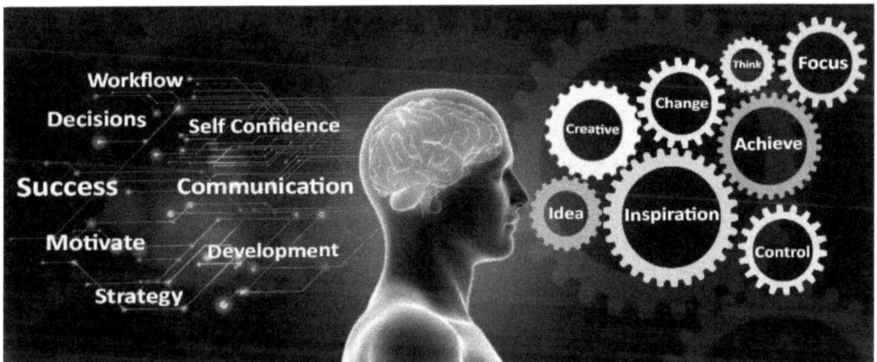

In certain aspects, manipulating the thoughts of others can be more straightforward than attempting to reprogram your own thinking. This is primarily because it's often easier to subconsciously influence someone without their awareness than it is to genuinely convince yourself of something you don't genuinely believe. It's crucial to remember that if you want to change someone else's mindset, you must have a well-defined approach. You need to understand what you're doing, how you're doing it, and why it matters. If you can accomplish this, you can effectively transform various aspects of another person.

In this chapter, we will explore the techniques for influencing others and the three key criteria to keep in mind when trying to alter someone else's mindset. Similar to reprogramming yourself, there are certain considerations to bear in mind. You can reshape their thoughts, narratives, or strategies, much like you can with your own, but the key is knowing what it takes to effectively program them.

Building Rapport

Building rapport becomes the cornerstone when it comes to programming others. Without establishing a strong rapport, your attempts to influence those around you will likely fail. A lack of rapport can lead to various complications in your relationships with others, undermining your influence.

We will delve into rapport development in the next chapter, providing a deeper understanding of how to achieve it to gain better control over your circumstances. Recognize that your ability to build rapport is pivotal in dealing effectively with others. When you establish that connection, you'll enhance your chances of success. It requires hard work, but your ultimate success greatly depends on it.

Rapport essentially functions as a way to disarm the unconscious mind, allowing you to bypass the conscious mind's defenses. It enables you to discover what truly matters and gain control over yourself and others' perceptions of you. Once you identify this "back door," you'll have the access and rapport needed for subsequent steps.

Understanding the Other Person

Next, you must focus on understanding the other person. What drives them? What motivates them? How can you gain insight into their thought processes? Can this understanding help you better handle the challenges you encounter?

When you comprehend the mental maps of others, you begin to understand their values, gaining the ability to interpret their thoughts, priorities, and concerns.

This skill is critical because without it, you won't know what needs to change. Essentially, it's about learning to read people and recognizing their actions and how they relate to the person you're trying to understand. This often involves tracing the individual's past actions and tendencies, allowing you to discern how to manage your understanding of them and, subsequently, their behaviors.

In essence, you're examining the thoughts, emotions, and behavior cycle to draw inferences about the other person, their mindset, and what you can anticipate from them. You must be prepared to analyze their body language, a nonverbal form of communication that reveals much about their inner thoughts. The sooner you master this skill, the closer you come to controlling their mindset effectively.

Body language serves as your gateway to explore the other person's unconscious mind, as it reflects unconscious communication aimed at influencing their actions and decisions. By focusing on this aspect, you can make informed decisions and gain valuable insights.

The connection between body language and emotions is undeniable. It serves as a direct link to the unconscious mind, emphasizing the need to establish a mutual understanding between the other person's unconscious mind and their outward expressions. To achieve this, it's crucial to pause and interpret their body language, deciphering the messages they are attempting to convey. Devoting time and effort to comprehending these non-verbal cues is essential.

Begin by analyzing their body language to discern their current emotional state. Is it open and welcoming, or closed and guarded? Evaluate whether their body language can be trusted or if it requires a reevaluation. Once you have a firm grasp of their body language, you can delve into understanding their emotional state.

Understanding their emotions allows you to piece together the bigger picture of their current situation. Observe the circumstances and triggers behind their feelings. This process enables you to gain insight into their thought processes, offering a comprehensive understanding of the situation. Recognizing their emotions also leads to identifying the underlying thoughts.

Remember that thoughts serve as the mental framework of an individual. By gradually comprehending the thoughts of others, you can better understand their behavior, recognizing patterns they may be unaware of or relying on your intuition to grasp the situation. Embrace this knowledge and contemplate how to utilize it effectively.

Ultimately, Neuro-Linguistic Programming (NLP) involves learning the inner workings of another person's mind. It entails adopting their perspective and comprehending their experiences, focusing on what truly matters and how to leverage this understanding. This capability is vital for altering the thought processes of others, leading to successful mindset changes.

Undoubtedly, this skill requires practice, foresight, hindsight, and empathy to develop a profound understanding of others. It may not always be easy or desirable to delve into someone else's mind. Nonetheless, gaining this insight into their perspective and thought processes is essential to navigate interactions effectively. This mastery of understanding allows you to harness NLP to reshape their thinking.

Guiding the other person's mind becomes possible once you have grasped a deep understanding of them. You realize that your interactions are intimately linked to how you perceive their thoughts. While you guide their mindset, it's crucial to respect the autonomy of their minds.

Nevertheless, there are instances when people benefit from having their thoughts guided, requiring a gentle push to gain better control over their thinking. When you can do this while maintaining respect for their individuality, you make choices that positively influence their minds.

Guide the Other Person's Mind

Ultimately, you must influence people with their best interests in mind. Identify areas within their current mindset that require change and implement these changes carefully to address the underlying issues. By doing so, you can shape the way you interact with them.

Begin by defining the goal you aim to achieve with them. Determine what needs to change within their mindset for their benefit. Recognize that understanding them is essential for success. Employ the techniques you will soon discover to implement your goal and witness the desired transformations.

10

RAPPORT

Establishing rapport is a fundamental aspect of any interpersonal relationship. Whether you are employing NLP techniques or not, rapport is akin to a gauge of your connection with another person. It represents your grasp of the intricacies that define their individuality and allows you to discern how best to bring about desired changes in those around you. When you cultivate rapport with someone, you forge a vital bond that shapes your interactions with them. This bond grants you the capacity to assert influence and maintain control over your engagements with the people in your vicinity.

Rapport extends beyond the art of subtly comprehending and persuading others. It transcends the mere outcome of having them follow your lead. It involves delving into the thoughts and emotions of another individual, fostering a relationship that binds you together, and gaining insight into the core drivers of their behavior. For any aspiring NLP practitioner, this understanding is invaluable. To master NLP for the benefit of others, one must effortlessly engage with people, work harmoniously with them, and diligently refine their ability to steer interactions.

What Is Rapport?

Rapport is the connection you establish with another person, a state in which both parties possess a deep mutual understanding. It's that feeling of effortlessly connecting with someone during a conversation, or having unwavering trust in the words and actions of those around you. It's recognizing the profound liking you have for someone you interact with. Rapport is a measure of the trust you develop for those in your social sphere, making it especially significant in the context of NLP.

At its core, rapport is a bond between two individuals, a sense of connection that compels you to react harmoniously with the other person. It involves sharing their emotions through empathy, experiencing their joy, comprehending their thought processes, and developing a genuine connection that fosters trust and authenticity in your relationships.

Typically, rapport is established through various means. Early on, it might involve discovering shared humor or compatible worldviews with the other person. It could even stem from shared experiences that lay the foundation for a strong bond. The rapport you build with another person is unique, potent, and indispensable, particularly in the practice of NLP.

Rapport and NLP

Rapport holds immense significance in NLP because it fosters trust and signifies the other person's attentiveness and belief in your credibility. This trust enables you to persuade and guide them through behavioral changes effectively, granting you the power to influence others successfully.

NLP relies on rapport because it operates at an unconscious level, without the subject's conscious awareness. People naturally trust and follow your lead when rapport is established. Think of how long-time friends walk together, maintaining the same pace and direction—this is the result of shared rapport. It ensures that individuals can synchronize their actions, trust each other, and guide themselves in harmony. When you establish rapport with someone, you essentially bypass their conscious defenses, earning their trust and making them more receptive to your influence.

This is often achieved through modeling, where you encourage the other person to mirror your behavior. You guide them to follow your lead, aiming to align their behavior with yours, ultimately increasing the likelihood of them following your lead.

Developing Your Own Connection

Building a connection with someone can occur organically over time as you spend time with someone you genuinely like, or it can be facilitated through deliberate methods. If you pay attention to your interactions with those around you, you'll notice that developing a connection naturally isn't a strenuous effort. It simply involves engaging with people on a meaningful level, seeking to establish a mutual liking. Being likable starts with being relatable, as it's easier to like someone who shares similarities with you, right?

However, there are instances when time isn't on your side, and you need to forge meaningful connections quickly. In such cases, you need to understand the art of connection-building. It's not too difficult to create these bonds if you know what you're doing. There's no shame in seeking guidance or assistance from others to enhance your skills. When you find yourself in need of that connection, you must discover a solution that works for you and ensures you can establish that connection when it's most crucial.

The most efficient way to build a connection is through mirroring. Mirroring allows you to accelerate the development of a connection, especially during a conversation when you and the other person are already in sync.

In essence, building rapport begins with mirroring, which is rooted in empathy. It involves activating those mirror neurons to make them work in your favor, enabling you to mirror someone effectively and encourage them to mirror you in return. Achieving this is relatively straightforward if you pay close attention.

To start, engage with the person you wish to mirror. Who are they? What are they engaged in? What's essential in your interaction with them? How can you facilitate this interaction? Identify their identity and engage in a conversation where they do most of the talking. By ensuring they're the primary speaker, you can nod in agreement while actively working to foster that connection. To do this, follow a few simple steps.

As the conversation progresses, ensure your body language signals that you're an attentive listener. Maintain eye contact, face the other person squarely, and nod in sets of three. This communicates your attentiveness, agreement, and recognition of common ground – a crucial foundation for rapport.

Next, focus on convincing yourself that you genuinely like them. Take the time to understand each other and relate on a personal level. When you establish this genuine connection or find the other person likable, you'll often discover that rapport naturally reciprocates.

When you engage in a conversation, pay attention to the other person as they speak. This natural engagement allows you to truly immerse yourself in the dialogue, leading to a better understanding and connection with them. But how can you ensure that you both end up in agreement? The most effective approach is to mirror their speech patterns. By mimicking their way of talking, you demonstrate your alignment with their perspective.

While some suggest mirroring body language, this can often come across as insincere or manipulative if not done subtly. It's crucial to avoid being seen as trying to force a point or manipulate others. To establish a genuine connection, your interactions with the other person should be smooth and unnoticeable.

When mirroring someone's vocal patterns, consider their tone, whether it's serious or cheerful, casual or formal. Try to match their general tone and vocabulary preferences for a successful connection. Additionally, pay attention to their speaking speed and attempt to mirror their pace to enhance the interaction's effectiveness.

Once you've mimicked their voice for a while, focus on identifying their "punctuator" – the specific gesture, phrase, or intonation they use to emphasize a point. This is their way of adding an exclamation mark to their speech. By mimicking their punctuator, you strengthen your connection with them, and they'll notice this shared connection.

Wait for an opportunity in your conversation where it seems they are about to use their punctuator, and then use it yourself. This will further cement the connection and rapport between you two. Their subconscious mind will recognize the bond, making your interaction more productive.

To test the success of your mirroring, make a small movement, such as brushing your hair or adjusting your posture, and observe if they do the same. If they mirror your actions, it indicates success. If not, consider trying again.

Establishing rapport may require multiple attempts, and if it doesn't develop after several tries, it might not happen at all. In such cases, you may need to explore other ways of connecting or let the rapport develop naturally. Remember, it's not just about making them feel the connection; it's also about experiencing it yourself.

11

UNDERSTANDING VISUAL, AUDITORY, AND KINESTHETIC CUES

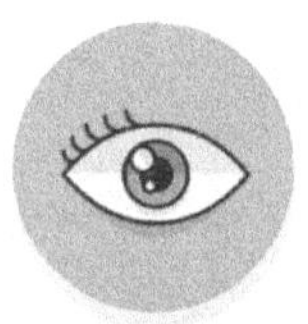

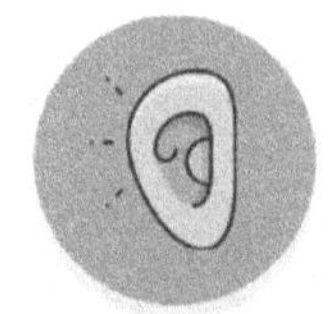

Before EMBARKING on your journey to explore NLP techniques, it's imperative to delve into the foundational principles of NLP's representational systems. These systems encompass the diverse learning styles inherent to each individual, with each person exhibiting unique methods of grasping information. Whether you're instructing children, adults, or any other demographic, it's crucial to remain attuned to these distinct learning styles. Broadly speaking, the three predominant modes of learning are visual, auditory, and kinesthetic. Your aim should be to align your teaching approach with these styles as closely as possible. By discerning an individual's preference within the VAK (Visual, Auditory, Kinesthetic) spectrum, you enhance your chances of effectively communicating with them.

Much like individuals vary in their learning preferences—some thrive through verbal communication, while others require written information or hands-on experiences—people respond differently to NLP techniques based on their unique styles. Identifying strategies to comprehend these diverse approaches allows you to gain deeper insights into their actions and influence them more effectively. Mastering this skill empowers you to engage, guide, and connect with others in unprecedented ways, and this book will equip you with the knowledge to achieve these goals.

Visual Learners:

Visual learners excel at absorbing information when they witness tasks or concepts being demonstrated. They grasp concepts more effectively by observing someone else's actions rather than relying on verbal explanations. To cater to visual learners, it is essential to model the desired behavior or skill for them. Establishing a strong rapport and physically demonstrating the desired actions is key. For instance, if you aim to help them overcome a habit like nail biting, you should intervene by redirecting their attention whenever they approach the behavior. Employing your body language can also influence their emotional responses by altering their nonverbal cues.

There are distinct indicators that can help you identify individuals with different learning preferences during your interactions. These preferences encompass visual, auditory, and kinesthetic learners:

1. Visual Learners:

- They speak rapidly and tend to jump from one idea to another, akin to a mental movie.
- They focus on the big picture when making decisions.
- In-person meetings are preferable to email or remote interactions.

- Their speech often has a higher pitch, and chest movements are noticeable during breathing.
- They maintain an upright posture and often look upward while visualizing.
- Gestures play a significant role in their communication.
- They are typically organized, neat, and well groomed.
- Written instructions are preferred over verbal ones.
- They frequently use expressions related to sight, such as "I see" or "I get the picture."

When interacting with visual learners, it's beneficial to use visual language and incorporate body language to engage them effectively.

2. Auditory Learners:

- Their behaviors and movements have a rhythmic quality.
- They speak in average tones and are sensitive to vocal nuances.
- Loud environments can be distracting for them.
- They excel at repeating information they've heard.
- They actively engage in conversations and are attentive listeners.
- Tilting their heads to the side is a common listening posture.
- They tend to memorize information in the order it's presented.
- Feedback through auditory channels is appreciated.
- Their breathing is centered in the chest.
- Expressions related to listening, such as "That clicks for me" or "I hear your side of things," are common.

To connect with auditory learners, engage in verbal communication, and employ persuasive techniques that resonate with their auditory preferences.

3. Kinesthetic Learners:

- They learn best through physical engagement and hands-on activities.
- Actions and movements are integral to their understanding.
- They speak slowly, with a deeper, resonant tone, and frequent pauses.
- Learning occurs through active participation.
- Physical contact serves as a valuable feedback.
- Comfort is a priority for them.
- They rely on intuition and gut feelings for decision-making.
- They position themselves closer to others during interactions.
- Active participation is essential for grasping concepts.
- They use metaphors related to touch in their speech, such as "getting a hold of someone" or "getting in touch."

To effectively communicate with kinesthetic learners, incorporate hands-on experiences and tactile elements into your interactions, as well as maintain physical proximity.

In conclusion, understanding these distinct learning preferences can enhance your ability to connect with others and tailor your communication to suit their styles.

When it boils down to it, your interactions with individuals you seek to influence and guide are closely tied to their sensory preferences. By prioritizing and consistently aligning with these preferences, you enhance your ability to connect with them effectively. If you can engage their preferred learning styles, it can significantly impact the success of your efforts to influence them.

If your attempts are successful, that's fantastic! However, if they aren't, it's crucial to identify what might be amiss and how you can adapt to improve the situation. Sometimes, a simple shift in perspective and adjustment of your teaching methods can bc the key to effectively reaching the other person. This is especially true if you are mindful of your own preferences and can recognize when you're defaulting to your own tendencies rather than considering their perspective.

12

NLP TECHNIQUES FOR YOURSELF

Now, let's take a moment to explore some of the most valuable techniques available in the realm of NLP that can assist you in reframing your perspective. These approaches typically enable you to better process your current situation with the aim of altering your mindset and, consequently, your experiences. By applying these methods, you'll notice a significant transformation in the way you engage with the world around you, ultimately contributing to your personal growth. In this discussion, we will delve into four key techniques that you can employ for your benefit.

Disassociation

Have you ever found yourself yearning to escape, as if you could simply vanish? This feeling often arises when you're enduring physical or emotional pain. Regardless of the type of distress, you instinctively wish to distance yourself from it, but your efforts seem futile. This is a common experience, but NLP can provide you with the tools to achieve just that.

NLP teaches you how to gradually disassociate yourself from the source of your discomfort. This technique is particularly useful, for instance, when dealing with a migraine. If it's your emotional state causing distress, you can apply the same principle, but ensure you adjust your self-talk accordingly.

Picture this: you're suffering from a painful foot injury, perhaps a sprained ankle from your morning jog. The pain is intense. Your objective is to create as much mental distance as possible between your mind and the pain to cope more effectively.

The process is straightforward. Begin by identifying the pain's location. Is it in your heart, head, or foot? Pinpoint the source, then focus on it momentarily. Ask yourself how it feels. What's the current sensation in your foot? How does your foot perceive the pain?

Undoubtedly, your foot hurts, but remind yourself that it doesn't possess thoughts or feelings—it's just a foot. Now, shift your attention slightly away from your foot. Inquire about your calf's reaction. How does your calf feel? Does it welcome the pain? How is it managing? Once again, you'll conclude that your calf is devoid of sensation or thought, lacking any perspective on the situation.

Continue this distancing process, moving progressively away from the pain in your foot. How does your thigh perceive your ankle's pain? What about your hip, stomach, back, and shoulders? Each step away from the foot's pain should further detach you from it, diminishing the suffering you're enduring. Extend this perspective shift to the world around you—how does the pain appear to others? How does it influence your behavior and interactions with the world? By the time you explore how the world perceives your pain, you'll often find yourself so distanced from the initial agony that it's no longer bothersome. You've either numbed the pain or eliminated it entirely, altering your thought process and narrative surrounding the ankle's discomfort.

Content Reframing

Content reframing is another exercise that can essentially reprogram your thought patterns. It teaches you to pause and view your thoughts from an entirely different perspective. This shift in perspective allows you to alter the content of your mind, subsequently transforming your thoughts, emotions, and behaviors.

We all carry internal narratives, but the key lies in your ability to completely reshape that narrative. Overcoming this narrative hurdle is where genuine progress and transformation in life begin. It empowers you to see the world in a new light. This visualization technique is especially beneficial for individuals who have experienced stress, abuse, or illness, serving as a means to alleviate trauma.

Content reframing typically occurs through one of two methods: altering the content or changing the context. In either case, you reframe the situation to better serve you. The outcome is a transformed interaction with the world around you, often leading to the resolution of your problems. Visualization practices can facilitate this process.

When altering the content, the goal is to change the meaning of the situation you're revisiting. You aim to shift your focus within the memory to something other than the primary issue. Shifting the context, on the other hand, involves redirecting your attention to something entirely different within the situation. You may reinterpret the situation positively, recognizing it as a valuable lesson rather than a problem.

To accomplish this, you should initially determine whether you're altering the content or the context. Next, delve into the depths of that traumatic memory. Reflect on the situation, immersing yourself in the memory. Picture the scenario vividly – envision yourself slipping in the mud during a rainstorm, feeling the embarrassment as your elementary school classmates dubbed you "muddy butt" for the rest of the year. It was a deeply humiliating experience, exacerbated by the persistent nickname. Since that day, you've noticed heightened anxiety during rain showers and a general unease when interacting with others, fearing vulnerability to future bullying.

To reframe this memory, pause and contemplate it. Visualize every detail of the incident – your fall, the mud-soaked pants, and the taunts from other children. Yet, in seeking a solution, divert your attention elsewhere. Reimagine the entire situation. Consider how it could have been worse – what if someone else had fallen or been injured? What if you had landed on someone else, causing harm? Explore the various ways the scenario could have unfolded and focus on a positive aspect – your mother picking you up, treating you to hot chocolate after cleaning up, resulting in more quality time together. This perspective shift can help reshape the memory.

By redirecting your focus from the negative aspects of the memory to a positive one, such as bonding with your mother over hot chocolate during rainy days, you realize that the situation wasn't as dire as it seemed. This shift enables you to move away from the victim mentality, concentrating on something meaningful and enjoyable. This change in focus improves your ability to process the situation and distance yourself from negativity.

Anchoring

Anchoring is an incredibly versatile technique in the realm of Neuro-Linguistic Programming (NLP). Essentially, it involves conditioning yourself to experience specific feelings or thoughts in response to particular actions. For many individuals, anchoring serves as a tool to manage anxiety or other stressors effectively.

When it comes to stress management, taming it is the ultimate goal. Imagine you frequently find yourself overwhelmed by stress, leading to panic when facing your tasks and responsibilities. This panic doesn't help you solve the problems at hand, but you can learn to combat it. The solution lies in the anchors you create. You simply need to select the anchors that suit you best.

If this concept sounds reminiscent of a high school psychology class, that's because it involves classical conditioning. Suppose you aim to conquer your anxiety. In that case, your goal is to associate feelings of calmness with stressful situations. As stress begins to escalate, identify a method to address the issue, and choose relaxation as your strategy.

With your anchoring method selected and your desired feeling (calmness) identified, you're ready to proceed. Recall a moment when you strongly experienced the emotion you want to connect with – in this case, calmness. It could be a memory of your wedding day or a serene night spent stargazing with your best friend. Regardless, focus on that memory until you begin to feel as calm as you did during that moment. Concentrate entirely on the sensation of calmness, and when it peaks, activate your chosen anchor – whether it's touching your necklace, tapping your hand, or making a specific gesture. Do this while you feel calm.

Repeat this process over several days. Every time you experience a strong sense of calm, use your chosen motion or gesture to anchor that feeling. Let yourself fully embrace it as you anchor it.

Over time, you'll notice increased calmness and improved well-being. You'll feel more confident that you've achieved what you set out to do. Test your anchor to see if it triggers those positive feelings. If it works, you've succeeded. If not, continue with consistency and persistence.

You can also link actions to your gestures, and with enough focus and effort, you can train yourself to accomplish almost anything. This is highly recommended; you should definitely attempt to utilize this technique. If executed correctly, it can help you overcome any negative emotions you might otherwise experience.

Belief Transformation

Finally, belief transformation is the last method we'll explore in this chapter. To change your beliefs, you need to start by acknowledging them. Remember that your existing beliefs are generalizations, and they may be entirely flawed, especially if they are negative and unhelpful. If you're burdened by negative beliefs, it's worth investing the time and effort to address them. You have the ability to pause, identify the negative belief, understand how it's problematic, and then take steps to make changes.

This shift in thinking is primarily about altering your thoughts. It involves simply correcting yourself when you notice that you're engaging in unhelpful negative thoughts. If these negative thoughts are hindering your ability to interact with the world positively, then it's imperative to change them. Correct them each time you catch yourself thinking these negative thoughts. Don't allow them to linger, and don't entertain them.

Erase these thoughts from your mind, and by the end of the day, you'll see progress. It all starts with changing one belief. As you consistently challenge and reprogram that initial thought, you'll realize something wonderful - you have the power to resolve the problem entirely. You can gain control over your thought patterns, which will enable you to cope more effectively with everything in your life.

13

NLP TECHNIQUES FOR OTHERS

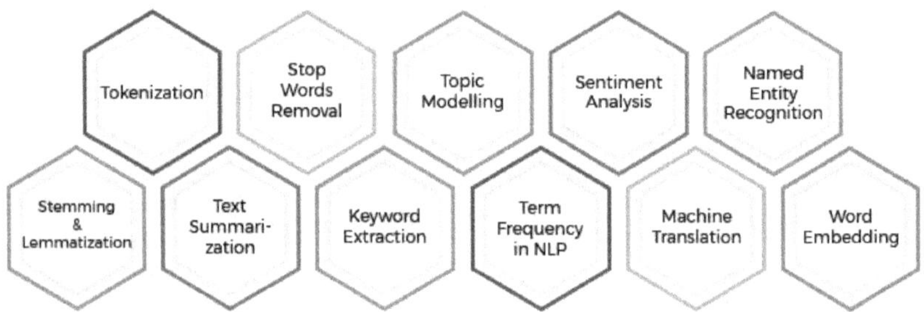

While this book doesn't primarily focus on portraying NLP as a form of mind control, it does offer insights into how it can directly shape the thoughts of those around you. The process is relatively straightforward. It involves engaging with others, subtly and subliminally interacting with their minds, and gradually influencing their reactions.

As previously mentioned, to effectively apply NLP techniques on others, you must prioritize building rapport. The key is to genuinely understand and gain the trust of the other person. Only then can you effectively utilize NLP techniques. Ultimately, confidence in your interpersonal interactions is essential for understanding how to exert influence.

In the following sections, we'll explore three straightforward methods to influence others' minds. These techniques aren't overly complex, but it's crucial to recognize that they also impact your own thought processes. The aim is persuasion rather than direct mind control, guiding others to perceive the world as you do.

1. Adjusting Speech Rate:

The heart rate range of 45 to 72 beats per minute is remarkably persuasive when delivering speeches meant to influence others. You can employ this pace to subtly suggest what others should think or feel. Simply slow down your speech to this rate, maintain gentle eye contact, and be attentive to your interactions. Recognize the power of this pace and how it encourages people to follow your lead.

2. Utilizing Sensory-Related "Hot Words":

Using "hot words" differs from conventional language use. It facilitates rapid and effective rapport-building based on how you communicate with others. These words typically relate to the senses since our sensory experiences shape our understanding of the world. This method is highly influential in communication.

Tailor your choice of hot words to align with the other person's preferred learning style. For instance, if someone is an auditory learner, emphasize auditory expressions and words, such as "hear me out" or "listen to my perspective." On the other hand, if someone is a kinesthetic learner, use touch-based language like "Feel free to notice..." or "Are you feeling it?" Shifting your language to align with their sensory preferences allows you to better understand and influence your interactions with them.

When considering that everyone possesses their unique sensory preferences, it becomes crucial to remind yourself of how to communicate effectively with those around you by distinguishing these sensory inclinations. Taking the time to understand and memorize these preferences is essential, as the ability to comprehend others' thoughts is a vital skill. Mastering this skill not only enhances your problem-solving abilities but also empowers you to influence people effectively by aligning with their sensory preferences. This skill is immensely potent.

Utilizing Your Body

The human body is remarkably persuasive. By mirroring someone's actions and subsequently guiding them, you can effortlessly alter their thought process. The key is to lead them skillfully. A common technique involves nodding discreetly while asking a question you want them to answer affirmatively. This subtle nodding, imperceptible to the other person, encourages them to nod in agreement. Remember, the unconscious mind is always observant, and this gesture resonates with it, increasing the likelihood of getting the desired response.

Pacing and Leading

Another technique to harness your body's influence is known as the "pace and lead" method. This approach entails matching the other person's body language before adopting it yourself. Essentially, you synchronize with their movements before taking the lead.

For instance, if you wish to lead a walk, start by matching the other person's pace, breath, and arm movements. As their mind detects this mirroring, you gain control. Gradually slow down the pace or alter your walking style, and observe as they naturally adjust to maintain the mirroring pattern. This technique empowers you to take charge of the situation effectively.

You can apply this principle in various contexts, such as guiding someone to agree with you or influencing their body language during negotiations, fostering a more receptive mindset. The possibilities are nearly limitless.

Utilizing Leading Words

Finally, consider employing leading words and phrases. These are akin to using "hot words," but instead, you rely on the fact that the other person will hear your suggestion and naturally respond to the question you've asked rather than the implied one.

Imagine a scenario where you want to plan a trip with your spouse. Instead of directly asking if they want to go, you inquire, "When should I purchase tickets for this event?" By framing your question this way, you bypass the need for explicit consent, and your spouse is likely to miss the implied request. This indirect approach increases your chances of obtaining the desired outcome without directly asking for permission.

14

CONCLUSION

Congratulations on reaching the conclusion of your journey through the realm of NLP (Neuro-Linguistic Programming). Hopefully, as you've traversed the pages of this book, you've gained a comprehensive understanding of how to harness these techniques for personal growth and transformation. You've learned how to not only reshape your own mindset but also influence the perspectives of those in your circle. Through NLP, you've discovered the means to assert control over your own thoughts and emotions, ensuring your ability to adapt and restructure your thinking, regardless of life's challenges.

The skills imparted within this book, centered on self-control and emotional mastery, are invaluable for everyone. Regardless of your background or circumstances, the power to manage your emotions is a precious asset that should not be relinquished lightly. You must commit to developing this skill effortlessly, and the most effective path to do so is by embracing NLP practices. These practices will empower you to realize that the changes you initiate can have a significant and tangible impact on your life. It's imperative to remember the profound utility of NLP, not just for yourself but also in its potential to influence those around you.

At this juncture, your primary task is to translate your newfound knowledge into meaningful changes in your life. It's time to take action and confront the challenges that may arise. You must grasp the mechanics of NLP and how they provide insights into what truly matters. Recognize the potency of your unconscious mind and how it can be harnessed, not only for personal growth but also to impact others positively.

These techniques can be employed to reshape your thought processes effortlessly or extended to assist others. Whether you aim to establish rapport, control the tempo of conversations, or persuade others to align with your desires, NLP offers a versatile toolkit. You can even use these methods to anchor yourself to a heightened sense of confidence in your daily life. NLP, in all its applications, holds the potential to be a transformative force for anyone fortunate enough to embrace it.

We extend our gratitude for investing your time in reading this book, and we wish you the best of luck in your future endeavors as you venture forth into the real world, armed with the wisdom imparted within these pages. Please bear in mind that these techniques wield substantial power, offering you the means to take charge of your own life and affect profound changes in the perspectives of those around you. Lastly, if you have found this book to be a valuable resource in any way, we would greatly appreciate your support in the form of an Amazon review.